This page was left intentionally blank

This page was left intentionally blank

This page was left intentionally blank

This page was left intentionally blank

This page was left intentionally blank

This page was left intentionally blank

This page was left intentionally blank

This page was left intentionally blank

This page was left intentionally blank

This page was left intentionally blank

This page was left intentionally blank

This page was left intentionally blank

This page was left intentionally blank

This page was left intentionally blank

This page was left intentionally blank

This page was left intentionally blank

This page was left intentionally blank

This page was left intentionally blank

This page was left intentionally blank

This page was left intentionally blank

This page was left intentionally blank

This page was left intentionally blank

This page was left intentionally blank

This page was left intentionally blank

This page was left intentionally blank

This page was left intentionally blank

This page was left intentionally blank

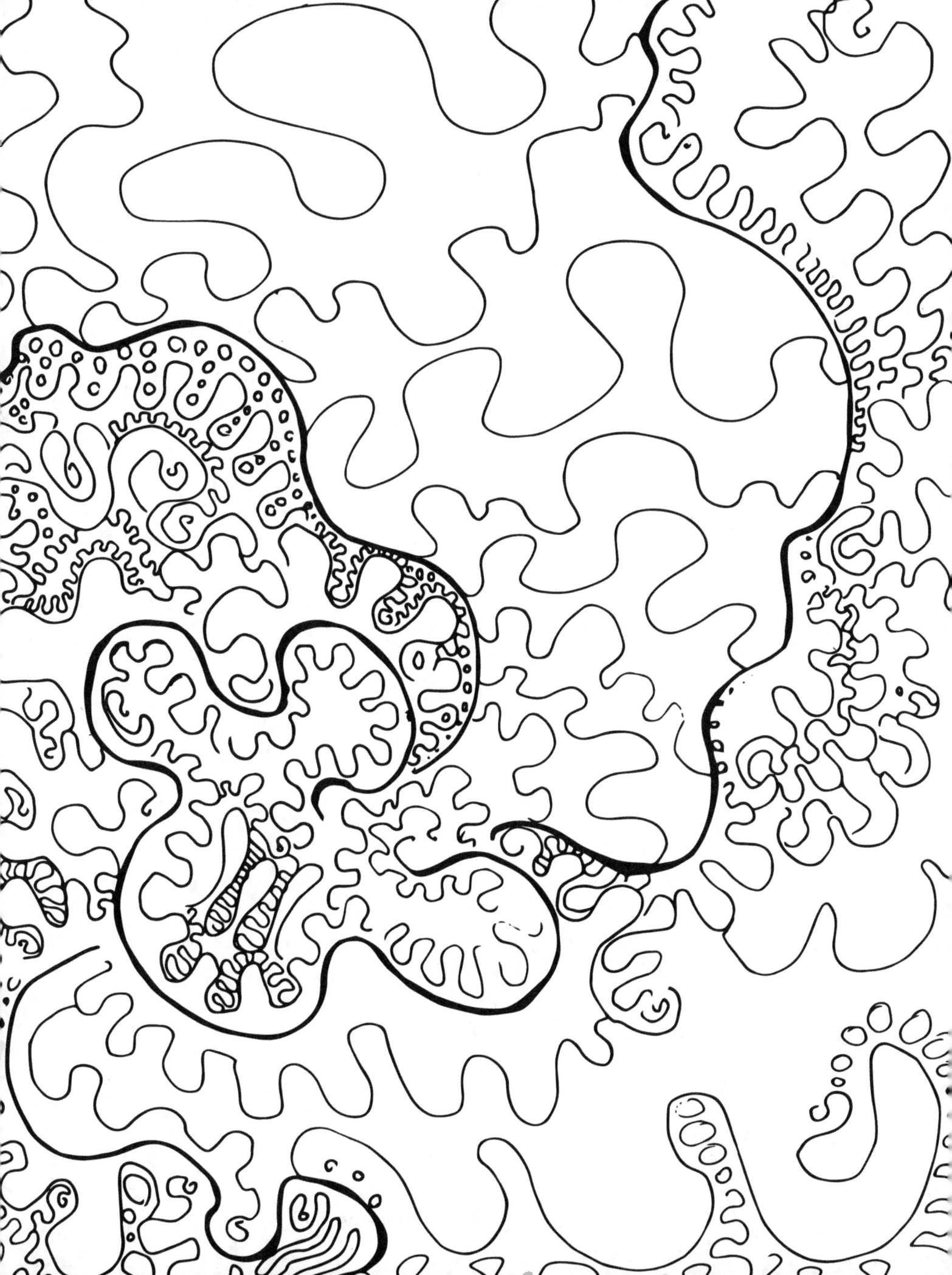

This page was left intentionally blank

This page was left intentionally blank

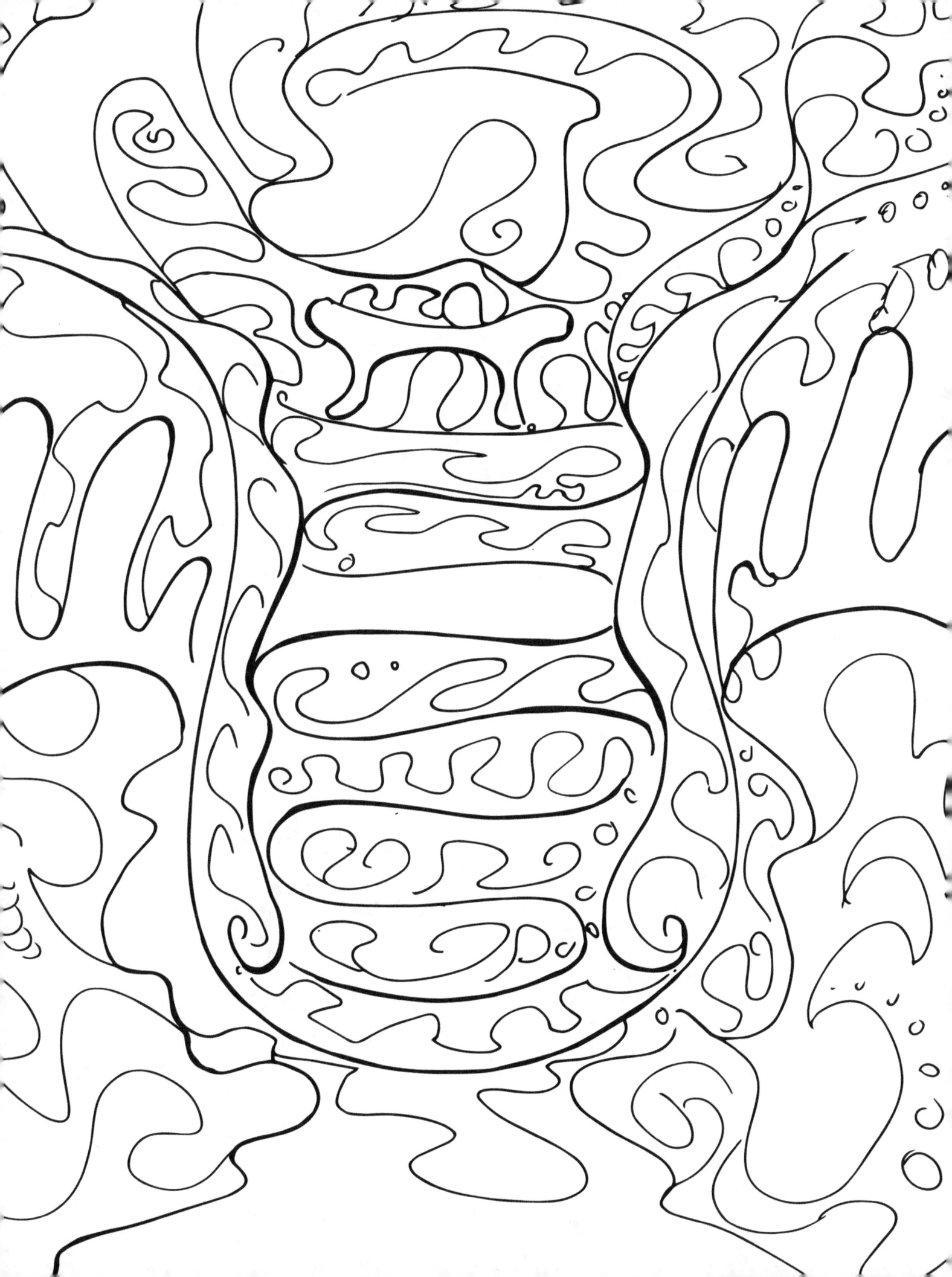

This page was left intentionally blank

This page was left intentionally blank

This page was left intentionally blank

This page was left intentionally blank

This page was left intentionally blank

This page was left intentionally blank

This page was left intentionally blank

This page was left intentionally blank

This page was left intentionally blank

This page was left intentionally blank

www.ingramcontent.com/pod-product-compliance
Lightning Source LLC
Chambersburg PA
CBHW081557280526

45788CB00011B/3499